the University College was established and gradually took over most of them, as well as the castle buildings.

The result is a city that would still be recognisable to one of the medieval pilgrims who journeyed to Durham to worship at the shrine of St Cuthbert. Nowadays tourists and students mingle in the narrow streets, but the bustle is good humoured and there is little traffic to distract from the rare atmosphere of the place. Paths drop through the trees from the cathedral and castle to join others by the riverside. Many people pause on lovely Prebends' Bridge to read Sir Walter Scott's words chiselled into a plaque on the parapet:

Grey Towers of Durham
Yet well I love thy mixed and varied piles
Half church of God, half castle 'gainst the Scot…

The Legacy of the Normans

The Legend of the Dun Cow

Durham is a magical place, so it is reasonable to use a little of this magic to unveil its origins. The mists of time part to reveal a crowd of people, many of them monks, attempting to shift a cart drawn by a pair of oxen. The cart is laden with a decorated shrine containing the body of St Cuthbert and has refused to budge for three days even though there is no obvious obstruction to its progress. One of the monks, Eadmer, is vociferous in explaining to his colleagues once again that it is Cuthbert himself who is stopping the cart from moving. The saint had spoken to him in a vision and insisted that his remains be taken to Dunholme to find a final resting-place and thus end more than a hundred years of wandering around the north of England, forever seeking to avoid the marauding Vikings. The only snag was that nobody knew of Dunholme.
As the monks and their followers become more and more exasperated with the immovable cart two women are seen approaching them seeking a lost cow. 'It may be at Dunholme', says one to the other. Eadmer overhears the remark and urges the others to follow the ladies, whereupon the wheels are miraculously freed and the party eventually reach Dunholme, a meadow at the top of a crag overlooking the densely wooded, steep-sided valley of the River Wear where the famous dun-coloured cow is quietly grazing.

ABOVE **Elvet Bridge**

BELOW **Dun Cow Sculpture, North Wall, Durham Cathedral**

St Cuthbert's body, with other treasures from Lindisfarne Priory, at first rested in a hastily-erected church built from scrubwood and roofed with turf. A more substantial timber church was followed by the building of a stone church on the Dunholme meadow dedicated on 4 September 999. This 'white church' soon became a place of pilgrimage as miracles attributed to St Cuthbert became more and more famous.

After the Norman Conquest the strategic importance of Durham was quickly recognised and in 1072 Waltheof, Earl of Northumberland, began to build a stone castle by the side of the 'white church' and the Benedictine monastery that had been founded by Bishop Walcher before his murder in 1080. He also girdled Durham with stone defence–works. The bishop's death triggered William the Conqueror's savage reprisal against the north that was organised from Durham. Walcher's successor, William of St Calais (or St Carileph),

continued establishing the monastery and decided to replace the 'white church', the foundation stone of the new one being laid on 11 August 1093.

ABOVE Palace Green and Durham Castle from the cathedral

Bishop William, who was also made Earl of Northumbria by William II, died in 1096 and was succeeded in 1099 by Ranulph Flambard, the first of the Prince Bishops, an energetic scoundrel who reigned for almost 30 years over the area that later became known as the County Palatinate of Durham. These lands, mainly between the rivers Tyne and Tees, were intended to act as a buffer zone between England and Scotland, where the warrior bishop's strong forces could act quickly to quell troublesome invaders from the north. However this strategy failed during the turbulent reign of King Stephen when King David I of Scotland joined forces with Matilda, Empress Maud, and forced King Stephen into conceding Northumbria. Pitched battles followed in the streets of Durham and the surrounding countryside before Henry II finally managed to restore order in 1157. His young nephew, Hugh of Le Puiset, Treasurer of York, had previously been appointed bishop, chiefly on the initiative of the Durham monks.

St Cuthbert was born c.633 and was a young shepherd when he dreamed of angels carrying a soul heavenwards. The next day he discovered that St Aidan, a missionary from Iona who founded Lindisfarne Priory on Holy Island, had died at the time of his vision. Inspired by this, Cuthbert joined the community of monks at Melrose Abbey and became Prior at the age of 30. His devotion to St Aidan then took him to Lindisfarne where he became renowned as a missionary and preacher. After ten years he withdrew from the community, preferring to live as a hermit on one of the Farne Islands with only seabirds and seals for company. Cuthbert returned to the mainland in 685 to be made Bishop of Northumbria, but after two years became ill and returned to his hermitage to pray and meditate, dying there on 20 March 687. In 698 his grave was opened and his body was found to be perfectly preserved. He was reburied in the oak coffin to be seen today at the cathedral, and almost immediately his sanctity was confirmed by miracles of healing.

LEFT St Cuthbert's Cross, Durham Cathedral

Medieval Durham

Le Puiset (whose name was soon anglicised to 'Bishop Pudsey' by locals) visited the Pope to have his appointment blessed, even though he was married and had three children. He returned to Durham determined to make the palatinate even more wealthy and powerful. His measures included granting a charter to the city's tradespeople, establishing his own mint at Durham, and encouraging pilgrims to come to the shrine of St Cuthbert. He also built hospitals and bridges in the city as well as the exquisite Galilee Chapel at the west end of the cathedral. He died in 1195.

By the middle of the 13th century Durham's identity as a city was becoming apparent with the great crossing tower of the cathedral completed to make the distinctive outline that we see today. One of the first written references to it concerns a fatal accident to a tightrope walker who failed in his attempt to walk from the central tower to one of the others. When Henry III heard of the incident he was furious with the Prior, telling him that he would never be promoted to the bishopric.

Throughout this time the relationship between prior and bishop was fraught, each disputing the other's authority. In addition the bishopric was under attack from the see of York, and in 1284 the Bishop was excommunicated by the archbishop, an order speedily overthrown by the King who thus endorsed the unique status of the palatinate.

In 1312 the Scottish army, led by Robert the Bruce, swept southwards and pillaged the city outskirts but failed to breach its walls. Soon afterwards Durham's defences were strengthened and in 1333 Edward III stayed at Durham on the course of a campaign against the Scots. The monarch paid homage to St Cuthbert by spending the night at his shrine, though his queen, Philippa, was forced to sleep at the castle as the monks said that Cuthbert had a dislike for women.

Medieval Durham must have been an eventful place to live – not only were the Scots on the warpath again in 1342 and 1346 (when they were routed at the Battle of Neville's Cross, about three miles from the centre) but the city frequently suffered from visitations of plague. In 1349 the Black Death reached Durham and took toll of its population for 18 months or so, while further epidemics of bubonic plague struck in 1416 and 1438. The economy of the city suffered from these outbreaks as rich pilgrims stopped coming to the shrines of St Cuthbert and the Venerable Bede.

By the beginning of the 16th century a citizen's life would have become more stable. Many were occupied in administering ecclesiastical and military needs while Durham's role as a market town became increasingly important. A guildhall had been erected on the Market Place in 1356 and most of the important trades were represented by guilds 150 years later.

BELOW **Stained glass window shows Edward III distributing money to local people in the Market Place, in gratitude for their loyalty (Town Hall)**

From the Tudors to the Commonwealth

King Henry VIII's quarrel with the church of Rome had serious consequences for Durham. When his commissioners rode into Palace Green in March 1538 the first thing they did was dismantle the shrine of St Cuthbert, thus depriving the city of a spiritual centrepiece that had brought it fame and prosperity for more than 500 years. Yet Durham could have suffered a worse fate – the monastic buildings were left standing and most of the monks were re-appointed as residentiary canons of the protestant church.

Within a few years grievances against the new order began to harden, and in 1569 the earls of Northumberland and Westmorland initiated the Rising of the North to support a restoration of the old religion. Their forces marched on Durham and the Roman mass was soon heard again in the cathedral. However, the rebellion collapsed when Spain failed to deliver the military support that had been promised. The earls fled to Scotland, their estates were forfeited and 500 of their followers executed.

The rebellion triggered other misfortunes. The countryside was impoverished by the fines levelled against landowners who had supported the revolt and in 1587 there was famine after the harvest failed. People already weakened succumbed to plague in 1589, and there were even worse outbreaks at the end of the century, with 844 people dying in Durham in 1597. At the same time Queen Elizabeth was taking revenge against Catholics, and several priests and laymen met their deaths at Durham, being hung, drawn and

ABOVE **Alms houses (Palace Green) dating from 1666, now used as a café/ restaurant**

quartered when they refused to renounce their faith. Gypsies were also persecuted, five being hanged in the city in 1592.

In 1601 the city was granted a charter by the Queen but the Bishop decided that it infringed his rights and refused to accept its legality. Instead he appointed one of his supporters as Mayor and drew up his own charter which gave Durham a limited say in its own affairs.

ABOVE **Memorial tablet, St Mary-the-Less Church**

LEFT **A view west over the towers of Durham Cathedral**

In 1643 Charles I was splendidly entertained by Bishop Morton at Durham en route to being crowned King of Scotland in Edinburgh. His next visit to the city four years later was a less joyous occasion. He passed through the city as a prisoner in transit to London and eventual decapitation. People in the city must have watched with mixed feelings for though much of the north was Royalist, there was also support for Cromwell in Durham, which strengthened when the Lord Protector abolished the bishopric and sold church property, including the castle. In 1650 3,000 Scottish prisoners, taken by Cromwell at the Battle of Dunbar, were held in the cathedral. With the restoration of Charles II to the throne most of the powers of the Prince-Bishop were also restored and Durham lost the democratic government it had enjoyed during the Commonwealth.

RIGHT
Framwellgate Bridge – rebuilt in 1401 with fortifications, long since removed

Durham since 1700

A turning point in Durham's history came in 1721 with the death of Bishop Crewe who had ruled the palatinate for nearly 50 years with most of the vice-regal powers still intact. At this time the city was beginning to assume its modern character with commodious houses being built for lawyers and merchants as well as even grander town residences for the gentry who occupied them during the 'season' of dances, theatre, and other events. Many of the local gentry had prospered from exploiting coalfields beneath their land. Fortunately for Durham the thin seams beneath the city were not worth working otherwise coaltips would have spoilt the scenery and subsidence threatened its buildings.

Over the years the bishop released more and more church land for these developments, and in 1832 he moved his palace from the castle in order that it could become part of the new university, the first to be founded in England after Oxford and Cambridge. This was endowed by the palatinate, initially as a theological college. In 1836 the ancient power of the Prince-Bishop was taken away and Durham became a normal diocese. At almost the same time the Municipal Reform Act established democratic local government, taking away the power of the guilds that had held sway since the medieval era.

Industry also took root in Durham. A woollen mill began working in 1780 but was soon converted into a carpet factory that proved more successful. Mustard milling and organ building were other important local industries, the latter surviving today with the firm Harrison and Harrison, founded in 1861.

Durham Today

Today Durham has a population of about 80,000 (compared with about 2000 in 1635). It is a thriving community centred on the university, county administration, and a busy shopping centre. Its wonderful cathedral and the other attractions of a beautiful ancient city mean that tourism is as important today as in the days when St Cuthbert's shrine attracted

LEFT **River Wear and lush riverside paths**

BELOW **Cathedral view from Framwellgate Peth**

crowds of pilgrims to Durham.

The city has also been undergoing some exciting changes. Millennium City is a £30 million major community, cultural and civic complex situated in the heart of the city, with craft workshops, the Tourist Information Centre and a large public square to be linked by a new footbridge to additional riverside parking and a new hotel. A new Visitor Centre will offer the first large-format film in Durham, taking visitors on an exciting journey through Durham's rich history. The centre-piece of the scheme – the 500-seat, multi-purpose hall has been named The Gala, to provide an echo of Durham's famous mining celebrations and to give a flavour of the top class entertainment which will take place there from January 2002.

The Castle

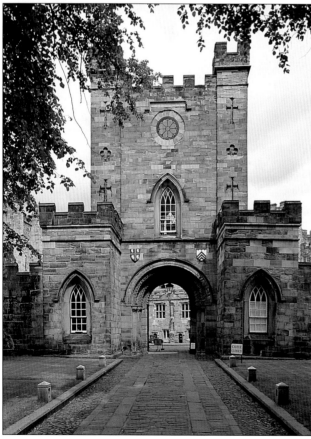

Durham Castle, with the cathedral that faces it on the other side of Palace Green, has been a World Heritage Site since the organisation was set up by UNESCO in 1986. It is acclaimed as one of the most perfectly preserved Norman fortresses in Britain, even though its buildings have served a variety of purposes over the centuries.

The priorities of the Normans when they arrived in a city was to set up a castle first, followed by cathedral and monastery. So it was at Durham with the first stronghold being constructed in 1072 by William I to aid his ruthless suppression of the northern rebellion. Shortly before his death he gave it to Bishop Walcher, the first of the Prince-Bishops of Durham.

At first the castle consisted of little more than a timber stockade on top of an earthen mound, but by the end of the century the stronghold had been expanded and a bailey built around the level ground to the west. A large hall was built by Bishop Flambard on the north side of the courtyard *c*.1120 which butted against the remarkable Norman chapel, which may have been built even earlier than the keep. Its roof is supported by six columns, their capitals decorated with primitive carvings of animals and country life.

One of the problems with the site was its lack of good foundations. Unlike the cathedral, which was mainly built on rock, the castle's foundations suffered from instability, especially the great west range magically perched high above the river. Over the centuries the defensive role of the castle became less important and it developed into a luxurious palace for the Prince-

Bishops. Visitors will be amazed by the enormous fireplace in Bishop Fox's kitchen (1499) and the exquisite woodcarving of the Black Staircase made for Bishop Cosin in the early 1660s. However, it is the Norman decoration that will linger in the mind longest, notably the doorway into Tunstal's gallery that is considered to be one of the finest examples of 12th-century stone-carving to be seen in England.

The University College of Durham came into being in 1836 and for many years was mainly devoted to theology, the students being housed in the castle. Today the university has far outgrown this site and new parts of the campus are sited on hills overlooking the city. Durham is the third oldest university in England, and can boast buildings that are more ancient than those at either Oxford or Cambridge.

ABOVE LEFT
Norman Chapel

ABOVE RIGHT
Ornately carved Norman doorway, the original external entrance from the courtyard

LEFT Durham Castle towering over the city centre

The city centre walk starts from the Market Place. A charter of 1180 gave formal permission for markets here, just outside the castle wall. St Nicholas' church was built in 1857, replacing a Norman one. The statue of Neptune once stood on a Pant where people drew their drinking water and the equestrian statue is of the third Marquess of Londonderry, d.1854, famous as a soldier and for

being an autocratic local mine-owner. With the church behind you bear left down Saddler Street (above). Many of the houses have 18th- or 19th-century façades disguising earlier origins. Turn left to drop down to Elvet Bridge (above), built c.1170 and widened 600 years later when

gatehouse, chapel and shops were removed. Elvet is said to derive from an Old English word meaning 'island of the swan'.

At the traffic lights cross to Old Elvet and pass the Royal County Hotel which incorporates 18th-century town houses and a temperance hotel. The red-brick Old Shire Hall (1895) now serves as the administration offices of the university. Opposite the Dun Cow Inn (above), its name taken from the legend of the founding of the city, turn right passing St Cuthbert's Catholic church on the right and the imposing Old Assize Courts (right) to the left – Durham prison is just behind them. The Courts were completed in 1807 but immediately had to be rebuilt, so shoddy was the original work. Pass the Court Inn and turn left at the main road and cross it at the traffic lights. A footpath on the other side of the crossing leads to Kingsgate Bridge, 1963, by Ove Arnup who also designed Sydney Opera House and the less successful Thames footbridge. Bow Bridge spanned the river here in medieval times.

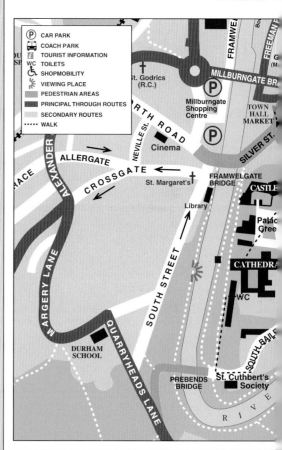

A Walk i

The walk (allow about one hour) beg
of the medieval city. Back on the p
There is a brief climb from the riverside
is made v

- (P) CAR PARK
- COACH PARK
- (i) TOURIST INFORMATION
- WC TOILETS
- SHOPMOBILITY
- VIEWING PLACE
- PEDESTRIAN AREAS
- PRINCIPAL THROUGH ROUTES
- SECONDARY ROUTES
- ····· WALK

St. Godrics (R.C.)
FRAMWE
FREEMAN
MILLBURNGATE BR
Millburngate Shopping Centre
TOWN HALL MARKET
RTH ROAD
NEVILLE St.
Cinema
SILVER ST.
ALEXANDER
ALLERGATE
CROSSGATE
St. Margaret's
FRAMWELGATE BRIDGE
CASTLE
Library
SOUTH STREET
ARGERY LANE
Palac Gree
CATHEDRA
WC
DURHAM SCHOOL
QUARRYHEADS LANE
PREBENDS BRIDGE
St. Cuthbert's Society
SOUTH BAIL
RIVE

On the other side of the bridge a cobbled lane joins the North Bailey at St Mary-le-Bow church (right), which is now the Durham Heritage Centre (see p.20). The original medieval church collapsed in 1637 and was rebuilt – the fine woodwork of this time survives. Turn left along the North Bailey (which

Durham

crossing the river into Elvet, a suburb
ula it follows the ancient defences.
e cathedral. A return to the Market Place
ce Green.

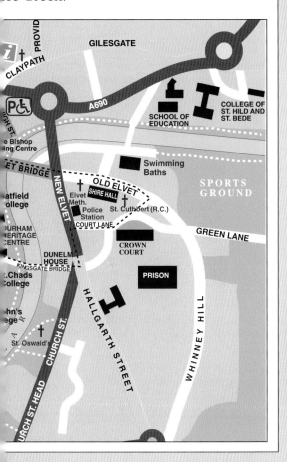

(below right) ends at a
picturesque arch built in
1778 on the site of the
Bailey Gate – you can see
a short length of bailey
wall on each side. Follow
the path towards
Prebends' Bridge (below
left), a viewpoint for both
the cathedral and the
river.

Do not cross the bridge but take a footpath to
the right that climbs the wooded slope to the
cathedral. Bear right again to go through metal

gates to the Dark
Entry (originally
a postern gate in
the defences)
and emerge into
The College, a
haven of peace
and beauty.

Turn left to follow a sign to the cathedral
restaurant (toilets to the left) and turn left into
the cloisters. Cross the nave of the cathedral

(see p.14) to the
north door
opposite that
opens on to
Palace Green.
The castle (see
p.10) is at the
far end. On the
right are the

Bishop's Hospital of 1666, founded by Bishop
Cosin whose magnificent hall (below) with its
foliated doorway is next door. To the left is his
Library (1669) with the Victorian University
Library next to it.

Go down Owengate in the far right corner of
Palace Green to rejoin Saddler Street. The great
North Gate of the abbey stood here until 1820
when the road
was widened for
stagecoaches.
Saddler Street
takes you back
to the Market
Place.

followed the outside of the city walls) and look
to the right through the former abbey gateway
for a view of The College
(top right), the Durham
name for the cathedral
close. Continue walking
into South Bailey and
pass St Mary-the-Less
church, which is the
chapel of St John's
College. Ancient
gravestones line its south
wall. The South Bailey

Durham Cathedral

The Norman master-mason at Durham truly put his faith on the line, trusting in the God who inspired his genius. Working more than 70 feet (22m) above the floor of the church, he spanned its width (39 feet, 11.89m) with slender ribs of stone, each rising transversely to meet at the centre. Then he filled in the panels between them with blocks of stone 18 inches (46cm) thick. When the blocks supporting the wooden scaffolding of the first bay were knocked away and the ceiling stayed in place he must have felt a surge of triumph as well as relief, and offered a thankful prayer to St Cuthbert. He had invented the vaulting which gives gothic churches their essential character, that soaring feeling that makes you feel that you are being pulled towards heaven.

No-one today can be certain where the revolutionary idea came from – most probably it belonged to William of St Calais, the bishop appointed by William the Conqueror to Durham in 1080. He was a Frenchman who travelled widely in Normandy, returning to lay the foundation stone of Durham Cathedral in 1093. He must have been an excellent fund-raiser and administrator as once work was started it continued energetically,

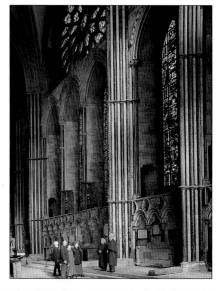

RIGHT **The Chapel of the Nine Altars with fine rose window**

BELOW **The Galilee Chapel containing the tomb of the Venerable Bede**

At the age of seven, Bede joined a new monastery at Monkwearmouth close to his home near Sunderland. His studious nature was quickly recognised by the Prior, a man who had travelled widely and collected books and music. After a few years another priory was founded close by at Jarrow and Bede was chosen to be one of the first monks. He stayed at Jarrow for the rest of his life (though he visited York and Lindisfarne), and his devotion and scholarship soon made the monastery famous throughout Europe. Bede not only studied theology but also wrote the definitive history of the first 700 years of Christianity in this country, which remains the most valuable source for early English history. He died in 735 and was buried at Jarrow until just before the Norman Conquest, when monks from Durham stole his bones and placed them in St Cuthbert's coffin. Both saints now have separate graves, at each end of the cathedral.

LEFT **Cathedral and Old Fulling Mill, now Durham University Museum of Archaeology (see p.20)**

BELOW **View from the High Altar**

even after his death in 1096. By 1099 the east end of the church and the transepts had been completed though the vaulting and the nave were only finished 30 years later. A remarkable feature of Durham – the enormous round pillars etched with zigzags and other motifs – are as many feet in circumference as in height (21 feet, 6.4m) and were constructed 'off site' and laboriously positioned with the help of primitive machinery.

The Galilee, or Lady, Chapel is at the west end of the cathedral and was finished in 1189. Its slender columns are a contrast to the massive ones in the body of the church and give the chapel its atmosphere of space and light. The tomb of the Venerable Bede is located in the Galilee Chapel, so called because it was the finishing stage of the Great Procession of Easter Day.

Originally the Lady Chapel was to occupy the eastern end of the cathedral but the bedrock was found to be unstable and the work transferred to the other end. In 1242 the Chapel of the Nine Altars was built on strengthened foundations so that all senior members of the monastery could say mass each day. Pilgrims and citizens who contributed

towards the building work were promised 30 days' remission of purgatory. Also at the east end of the church is the Neville Screen. This must have been overwhelming when it was consecrated in 1380. Gilded and painted in bright colours, its niches were filled with 107 alabaster figures.

Outside the castle wall

Durham's site was ideal for defence but presented problems for ordinary citizens in medieval times who needed to work and trade in the city. The unique amalgam of monastery and castle at the heart of the city under the rule of worldly, powerful bishops inevitably meant that the interests of humble tradespeople were usually ignored.The Cathedral and castle were enclosed by well-guarded gates and walls, and there were also gates on both main bridges.

Archaeologists believe that there was a settlement here before the arrival of the monks with St Cuthbert's remains. In Saddler Street, just outside the original fortified area, they excavated timber structures which proved to be the premises of various tradesmen, amongst them a potter, shoemaker, wood-turner, fishmonger and butcher. From these beginnings trade expanded through the ages so that the city soon outgrew the peninsula, four boroughs and a barony being created to encircle the city. These had their own churches and operated more or less as parishes, with the bishop as lord of the manor taking dues from facilities such as the local mill and communal bakehouse. The revenue from the Borough of St Giles, on the north-eastern fringe of the medieval city, was given to the hospital founded there by Bishop Flambard in 1180.

Human nature being what it is, citizens adapted their lives to the regulations of their overlords, trying all the time to overturn the more irksome ones. Since clergy and their soldiery were dependent on provisions and services from outside the defences it was in their interest to

ABOVE **The Market Place bordered by the Town Hall and St Nicholas' Church**

RIGHT **St Margaret's Church**

be flexible, and on the whole the system seems to have worked reasonably throughout the Middle Ages. Until the early 14th century the market place was outside the walls, but then the defences were extended to the north to include it with St Nicholas' church (rebuilt in 1857).

The face of Durham changed in the 18th and 19th centuries. Development took place in the centre of the city where the massive North Gate at the south end of Saddler Street was demolished while in the Market Place the Guildhall replaced The Tollbooth that had served as a town hall for 200 years. In 1848 the Guildhall was in turn replaced by the present Town Hall with the indoor market taking the former site of the Earl of Westmorland's town house next door.

Expansion was transforming the outskirts of the city too. A new Court House and prison were built in Elvet, the latter necessary as the North Gate had previously served as Durham's gaol. On the opposite (western) side of the city development was spurred by the railway while to the north much new housing was built around Gilesgate.

ABOVE **Magnificent stained glass window, Town Hall**

LEFT **Indoor Market stallholder**

Durham University

After its foundation in 1832 the initial growth of the university was unhurried. Teaching was restricted to theology and, remarkably, astronomy with students following a collegiate life on the models of Oxford or Cambridge. The university was confined to the peninsula for almost 100 years, the first surge of expansion beyond the city walls only coming in 1924 when science laboratories were built on South Road. Before this, in 1908, re-organisation had seen Durham amalgamated with Newcastle where sciences and medicine had been taught since the 1850s.

This arrangement lasted until 1963

when Newcastle became a university in its own right. This meant that Durham had to establish its own science departments in new buildings. At the same time arts faculties joined administrative offices in the Old Shire Hall, newly vacated by the county council. The Kingsgate footbridge was built to link this part of the university with the original foundation based on castle and former monastic buildings.

The expansion of universities in the 1960s and 70s saw Durham grow into a fully-fledged modern seat of learning. Today there are 11 colleges, five on the peninsula, accommodating nearly 12,000 students. A wide range of subjects are taught in the 31 departments and the cosmopolitan outlook of Durham is underlined by a satellite college of Teiyko University, Japan, which was founded on the campus in 1990.

Two of Durham's tourist attractions are on the university campus, on each side of South Road. The Botanic Garden covers 18-acres and has a tropical house, rare trees from the Far East, sculptures and a tearoom. The Oriental Museum stands opposite the Teiyko University building on the west side of South Road and has an important collection of Oriental antiquities and art.

The Little Count

Count Jozef Boruwlaski was born in Poland in 1739, one of six children, three of whom were of normal size. Jozef, his sister and a brother grew to be little more than three feet tall. He was cared for by a succession of aristocratic families after the death of his father when he was ten. Jozef showed talent as a musician and was sent to Paris to learn the violin, and in his teens toured the courts of Europe where he found favour with the 16-year-old Marie Antoinette who gave him her ring. In 1781 he secretly married the companion of the countess who cared for him, and was banished from her palace when the wedding was discovered. In the following year the Count was in London and became friendly with the Prince of Wales (later George IV). He continued to travel, visiting many of the great houses of England and Ireland. By 1791 his wife and children had become tired of this nomadic life and deserted him. In his memoirs the Count wrote of his relief at this. When she became exasperated the Countess would lift him on to a mantelpiece and leave him stranded there.

Some of his closest friends lived in Durham and in 1791 he decided to settle there, living in a residence called Calamano House which used to stand near Prebends' Bridge. Here his days 'glided on in undisturbed tranquillity', though as he grew older he suffered from being teased by the choirboys who used to pull his long hair. When he came to Durham he had purchased an annuity from a local shopkeeper who believed that the Count, like most dwarves, would have a short life. In fact he lived to be almost 98 and outlived the shopkeeper (who he enjoyed teasing about his investment). Count Boruwlaski is buried in the cathedral, an unobtrusive stone carved with his initials marking the spot close to the Galilee Chapel.

LEFT **Portrait of Count Boruwlaski (Town Hall)**

ABOVE **Statue of 'The Little Count' (Town Hall)**

BELOW **The 'Count's House', actually a Victorian folly near the site of his home (now demolished)**

Other attractions

The River Wear has been vital to Durham through the ages, creating its natural defences and giving the city its unequalled scenic character. This can be appreciated from the walks that criss-cross the woodland on both shores, and you could spend the best part of a day exploring them. If you do this you will also discover the **Durham University Museum of Archaeology**, housed in a picturesque fulling mill below the cathedral. Its exhibits illustrate the early history of Durham and the surrounding area.

Boat hire and river trips are always popular with visitors who may find it more energetic than anticipated to row from Elvet Bridge to the weir above Prebends' Bridge. The lazy, but equally pleasant, option is to take a boat cruise in the other direction, which takes about an hour. Each June 600 or so crews take part in the **Durham Regatta**, the second oldest in the country.

The **Durham Heritage Centre** in the former St Mary-le-Bow church in North Bailey has a wide-ranging display that sheds light on

RIGHT **Crook Hall and gardens**

BELOW **Durham Miners' Gala**

BOTTOM **Durham Regatta**

some little-known aspects of Durham's history. A cell similar to one in the Durham Prison of today is compared with the facilities that prisoners enjoyed if they were locked in a dungeon of the North Gate, the city's first gaol.

Downstream from the city centre, at Sidegate is **Crook Hall**, a 14th-century manor house set in four acres of beautiful gardens, most of them designed to a theme. The **Durham Light Infantry Museum** occupies brand-new premises at Aykley Heads. The famous regiment's history is the major subject of the museum, but the experiences of the civilian population of the city during the Second World War are also shown while the Art Gallery holds travelling exhibitions as well as ones by local artists.

Finchale Priory (English Heritage) is four miles from Durham, the romantic ruins of a 12th-century Benedictine monastery in a riverside setting. Monks from Durham used to come out in relays to spend holidays here and its founder, St Godric, was 105 when he died in 1170.

ABOVE St Oswald's Church, located on the site of an Anglo-Saxon church, one of the heritage attractions in the city

RIGHT Finchale Priory

BELOW RIGHT Durham Light Infantry Museum

Choral Evensong in the cathedral is an event that will linger in the memory of those who attend. Once a year, usually on the day of the Friends' festival in early June, the cathedral choir climb the 325 steps to the top of the tower to sing. Originally this was to give thanks for the English victory over the Scots at the Battle of Neville's Cross in 1346. The singing commemorated monks singing from the tower at the time of the battle. The choir sing on two sides of the tower.

The most famous event in the city is the **Miners' Gala** that takes place on the second Saturday in July. Although mining is no longer a part of the local economy, former miners still carry their union banners through the streets to a service in the cathedral, and brass bands ensure that it is a noisy as well as a colourful spectacle.

The surrounding area

BELOW **Raby Castle, Staindrop**

FAR RIGHT **'The Town', Beamish Museum**

BOTTOM **Auckland Castle, Bishop Auckland**

Durham lies at the heart of countryside where wild moorland merges with an area that was involved with many of the inventions vital to the Industrial Revolution.

Raby Castle is close to Staindrop about 15 miles south-west of Durham. The moated stronghold was built for the Nevill family in the 14th century,

but their estates were forfeited after the disastrous uprising of 1569. In 1626 Raby was leased by Sir Henry Vane, James I's Secretary of State, and his successors have lived there ever since, remodelling the castle over the centuries. The castle remains one of the most romantic in England, and has a magnificent park. The medieval character survives even though Raby has undergone much change – the highlight of the interior is the Octagon

Drawing Room, just one of the rooms where old master paintings are displayed along with equally magnificent furniture.

Auckland Castle, the palace of the Bishop of Durham, was the country retreat of the Prince-Bishops where they would entertain guests and take them hunting – there is still an 800-acre deer park. In spite of its pinnacled appearance outstanding medieval architecture is to be seen inside, including the chapel (reputedly the largest private chapel in Europe) which was the original banqueting hall. The Long Dining Room has a famous set of paintings of Jacob and his Seven Sons chosen for it by Bishop Trevor in 1756 while the King Charles Dining Room has wonderful plasterwork. There is an exhibition on the life of St Cuthbert in the former kitchens.

The Beamish Open Air Museum is a unique museum illustrating the way life used to be lived by local people at two points in time, 1825 and 1913. Regular services of trams, old motor cars, and horse-drawn vehicles take visitors to various parts of the site where they can see a colliery village,